The Antarctic Treaty

Julie Haydon

ANTARCTIC TREATY
TRAITÉ SUR L'ANTARCTIQUE
Договор об Антарктике

Rigby®

www.Rigby.com
1-800-531-5015

Rigby Focus Forward

This Edition © 2009 Rigby, a Harcourt Education Imprint

Text © 2008 Julie Haydon
Published in 2008 by Nelson Australia Pty Ltd ACN: 058 280 149
A Cengage Learning company

1 2 3 4 5 6 7 8 374 14 13 12 11 10 09 08 07
Printed and bound in China

The Antarctic Treaty
ISBN-13   978-1-4190-3842-6
ISBN-10   1-4190-3842-7

Acknowledgments
The author and publisher would like to acknowledge permission to reproduce material
from the following sources:
Photographs by Auscape/ Still Pictures, p. 21; The Art Archive/ Global Book Publishing,
p. 6; British Antarctic Survey/ Chris Gilbert, p. 13; Corbis/ Kit Kittle, p. 18; Getty Images/
AFP, front cover bottom, pp. 1 bottom, 17/ Hulton Archive, p. 8/ Kim Heacox, p. 4;
National Library of Australia, p. 7; Newspix/ KH Mackenzie, p. 9; Photolibrary/ Chris
Sattlberger, p. 19/ BAS, back cover, p. 14/ Doug Allan, p. 20/ Geoff Renner, p. 22/ Photo
Researchers, p. 23/ Rick Price, front cover top, pp. 1 top, 16/ SPL, p. 5

The Antarctic Treaty

Julie Haydon

Contents

Chapter 1

ANTARCTICA

Antarctica is the fifth-largest continent on Earth. It is also the coldest, windiest, driest, and highest continent. It is an ice-covered place where no large plants grow and no land mammals, reptiles, or amphibians live.

Antarctica covers an area of more than 5.25 million square miles. It is one-and-a-half times the size of the United States or nearly twice the size of Australia.

an Antarctic research base

Antarctica does not belong to one country, and it has no government. People visit Antarctica—usually as tourists or to do scientific research—but no one lives there all the time.

Chapter 2

DISCOVERING ANTARCTICA

Antarctica was the last continent to be discovered. It is not certain who first saw Antarctica, but sailors began to map Antarctica's coast from their ships in the 1800s. The first confirmed landing was in the mid-1890s.

Over the next few years, several men tried but failed to reach the South Pole, which is Earth's southernmost point.

a map of Antarctica from the mid-1800s

Finally a team led by Norwegian Roald Amundsen reached the South Pole in 1911. By then countries around the world were becoming more and more interested in the frozen continent. Soon seven nations—Argentina, Australia, Chile, France, New Zealand, Norway, and the United Kingdom—had laid claims to parts of Antarctica.

Roald Amundsen and his dogs at the South Pole

Talk of a Treaty

Because so many nations had made a claim to territory in Antarctica, it was clear that fighting might break out. **Diplomats** from different countries wanted to stop a war from starting, so they began talking about a treaty for Antarctica. A treaty is a written agreement signed by two or more nations.

A U.S. Navy member makes a trail across the Antarctic.

Several countries had already set up research stations in Antarctica where scientists could live and work. Most scientists worked during the summer months when it was not as cold as in winter. Scientists hoped a treaty would allow them to continue their work and to exchange information with scientists from other countries.

Chapter 3

THE ANTARCTIC TREATY

In 1959, 12 nations signed the Antarctic Treaty. The nations were Argentina, Australia, Belgium, Chile, France, Japan, New Zealand, Norway, South Africa, the Soviet Union, the United Kingdom, and the United States. The treaty went into effect in 1961.

Aims of the Treaty

One of the aims of the Antarctic Treaty was to put on hold all claims to territory in Antarctica. So although no nation gave up its claim to territory in Antarctica, the nations agreed not to take any further action. Instead people from the treaty nations would coexist peacefully while in Antarctica.

A scientist studies Antarctic weather, using a weather balloon.

Another aim was to promote scientific research and international scientific cooperation. The treaty nations agreed that it was in the interest of all humans that scientific research in Antarctica continue and that scientists from different countries help one another.

Still another aim was to protect the Antarctic environment, including Antarctica's plants and animals.

In the Antarctic Treaty, the nations agreed that:

- Antarctica shall be used for peaceful purposes only.
- freedom of scientific research in Antarctica shall continue.
- scientific information and personnel shall be exchanged between countries.

- nuclear explosions and the dumping of radioactive waste is not allowed in Antarctica.
- inspections of any nation's stations, equipment, supply ships, airplanes, and helicopters are allowed.
- there shall be freedom of access to all areas of Antarctica.

Over the next twenty years, other agreements were created that supported the Antarctic Treaty. These agreements went into more detail about the **conservation** of Antarctica's animals and plants.

The treaty has been a huge success. There has never been a war in Antarctica, nations cooperate while doing important scientific research, and there are rules in place to protect Antarctica's environment. Today 46 countries have signed the Antarctic Treaty.

The countries that have signed the Antarctic Treaty are:

Argentina	Ecuador	Poland
Australia	Estonia	Republic of Korea
Austria	Finland	Romania
Belarus	France	Russian Federation
Belgium	Germany	Slovak Republic
Brazil	Greece	South Africa
Bulgaria	Guatemala	Spain
Canada	Hungary	Sweden
Chile	India	Switzerland
China	Italy	Turkey
Colombia	Japan	Ukraine
Cuba	Netherlands	United Kingdom
Czech Republic	New Zealand	United States
Democratic People's Republic of Korea	Norway	Uruguay
	Papua New Guinea	Venezuela
Denmark	Peru	

Chapter 4

THE MADRID PROTOCOL

An important issue that was discussed by the treaty nations in the 1980s was whether mining should be allowed to take place in Antarctica. Some countries thought that it may be possible to mine valuable minerals in Antarctica while still protecting the Antarctic environment. However, some countries did not want any mining to take place. This led to talks about better ways of protecting the Antarctic environment.

In 1991 the Antarctic Treaty nations signed an agreement called the Madrid Protocol. A protocol is a document that is added to a treaty and that includes information having to do with the treaty. The protocol went into effect in 1998 and called Antarctica a natural reserve devoted to peace and science. It set strict rules to protect the Antarctic environment.

ANTARCTIC TREATY

TRAITÉ SUR L'ANTARCTIQUE

ДОГОВОР ОБ АНТАРКТИКЕ

MINISTRA DE MEDIO AMBIENTE

PRESIDENTE

treaty members meeting in Madrid in 2003

The Madrid Protocol:

- banned mining in Antarctica.
- set strict rules for waste storage and disposal.
- banned bringing nonnative species of plants and animals into Antarctica without a permit.
- set rules to help reduce marine pollution.
- said that nations must make plans to prevent and deal with an environmental emergency.

Chapter 5

LIVING IN ANTARCTICA

There are now more than forty research stations, run by many countries, in Antarctica. The people who live and work at the stations must live by the rules set out in the Antarctic Treaty and the Madrid Protocol.

Polish research station on King George Island, Antarctica

It is not only scientists who work in Antarctica. Engineers, mechanics, carpenters, plumbers, electricians, doctors, chefs, and station leaders also work at the stations. There are no stores in Antarctica, so everything people need to live and work there must be brought in, usually on large ships.

Scientists in Antarctica

Scientists go to Antarctica to study many different areas of science. Biologists study Antarctica's animals, while botanists study Antarctica's plants. Meteorologists study the atmosphere and weather, glaciologists study Antarctica's ice, and geologists study Earth's crust in Antarctica and beneath the Southern Ocean.

A scientist tags a Weddell seal.

Oceanographers study the Southern Ocean, while medical researchers study what living in Antarctica does to the human body.

Scientists lower a device to measure the pressure on the seabed.

Chapter 6

TOURISTS IN ANTARCTICA

A small number of tourists visit Antarctica each year. Most arrive on ships that are owned by tour companies. Tourists must also obey the rules set out in the Antarctic Treaty and the Madrid Protocol.

For example, tourists must not leave garbage or disturb animals or plants. They must obey safety rules and get permits to visit protected areas, and they must not disturb scientific research.

Glossary

conservation   protection of the environment and the creatures that live within it

diplomats   people appointed to represent a government in its dealings with other countries

Index